THE
MARGARITA
GUIDE

THE MARGARITA GUIDE

cocktails for every occasion

=== Steve Quirk ===

NEW HOLLAND

CONTENTS

Introduction 7

Margarita Cocktails 23

Glossary 136

Index 140

Introduction

You now have 50 Margarita cocktail recipes at your fingertips, from basic mixers through to exotic creations and will never be short of a Margarita recipe again. Check out the useful tips on preparing for hosting your own Margarita parties where you can take your guests on a cocktail journey to remember. Each recipe has clear and uncomplicated directions – even those with no previous cocktail-making experience will be easily creating delicious Margaritas.

A Margarita is traditionally a Tequila-based cocktail although there are a few Margarita cocktails in this book that are Rum and Vodka-based.

Approximate % alcohol volume (% alc/vol) content has been calculated and supplied for each drink in this book, as well as how many standard drinks each contains. These calculations are based on information obtained that is believed to be accurate and reliable, although they cannot be guaranteed due to % alc/vol variations between the different brands of spirits and liqueurs. These calculations should only be used as a guide.

The % alc/vol for all spirits and liqueurs required for drinks contained within this book are provided in the glossary – if unsure then compare your spirits and liqueurs with the % alc/vol provided in the glossary.

◆ CONSTRUCTING A MARGARITA ◆

Shaking – When ingredients require shaking, half-fill a cocktail shaker with ice, and then pour ingredients into the shaker over ice. This will chill the ingredients quicker than pouring the ingredients into the shaker before ice. Avoid over-filling your shaker – leave room for shaking. To shake, stand still and shake vigorously for about ten seconds, strain into your chosen glass and serve or garnish. The majority of cocktail shakers have a strainer; if yours does not then you can use a Hawthorn strainer. Effervescent drinks should never be shaken in a cocktail shaker. Rinse the shaker out thoroughly after each use and dry with a clean lint-free cloth. This will ensure that your drinks only have in them what they are supposed to and will not distort the flavour of the next drink that you prepare.

Stirring – Where ingredients are required to be stirred, half-fill a mixing glass with ice and pour the ingredients over the ice. Stir and strain into chosen glass. Usually ingredients that mix easily together are prepared in this manner.

Layering – To layer a drink is to pour ingredients in order given (pour over the back of a spoon into chosen glass). This will allow the liquid to flow down the inside rim of glass, creating a layering effect. Usually the heavier ingredients are poured first.

Blending – When a blender is required, only use cracked or crushed ice in suitable blenders and blend until ingredients are evenly mixed. Margarita cocktails should be drunk as soon as they are served.

◆ USEFUL TIPS ◆

Frosting – This is for the purpose of coating the rim of a glass with salt or sugar. This is achieved by moistening the rim of a glass using a slice of lemon or orange. Then hold the chosen glass by its base or stem upside down and rest gently on a flat plate containing salt or caster sugar and twist slightly. If you press down on glass too hard, this may result in chunks of salt or sugar sticking to the rim of glass. Lemon is used for salt-frosted rims and orange for sugar-frosted rims unless otherwise stated.

To chill a glass – Glasses can be chilled by placing them in a refrigerator or by placing ice cubes into the glasses while drinks are being prepared. Discard these ice cubes before pouring unless otherwise instructed.

Sugar syrup – To make sugar syrup, bring one cup of ordinary white sugar with one cup of water almost to the boil in a small saucepan stirring continuously and simmer until the sugar is completely dissolved. Then remove from the heat and allow to cool. Once cool, pour into a resealable container or a corked bottle and store in the refrigerator or behind your bar for regular use. This syrup will now last indefinitely.

Sweet & sour mix – To make sweet & sour mix bring one cup of sugar syrup to the simmer then add ½ cup fresh lemon juice and ½ cup fresh lime juice. Simmer till well mixed stirring frequently, then remove from heat and allow to cool. Once cool, pour into a resealable container or corked bottle and store in refrigerator for up to ten days. Sweet & sour mix is also referred to as sour mix or bar mix.

Fruit, peels and juices – Fruit slices and pieces will keep fresher and longer if covered with a damp clean linen cloth and refrigerated. Where citrus peel is required, cut the peel into required sizes and shave away the white membrane. Fruit and peels should be the last ingredient added to a cocktail (garnish). When juices are required remember – fresh is best. When using canned fruit and/or juices, transfer the can's contents into appropriate resealable containers and refrigerate.

Ice – It is important to maintain a well-stocked clean ice supply, as most Margarita cocktails require ice during construction. To obtain crushed ice, if you do not have access to an ice-crushing machine, place required ice onto a clean linen cloth and fold up. Place ice-filled cloth onto a hard surface and smash with a mallet (not a bottle).

◆ GLASSWARE ◆

Glasses come in a wide variety of shapes and sizes and range in value depending upon the quality of glass. When washing glasses, use hot water without detergent as detergent can distort the flavour of a drink or reduce the fizz in an effervescent drink. Only wash one glass at a time and dry with a clean lint-free cloth. Before using a glass, give it a quick polish with a glass cloth and check glass for chips and/or cracks. When handling glassware, hold glasses by their base or stem, as this will avoid finger marks around the rim of glass, thus maintaining a high polish.

The following is a list of glassware required for Margarita cocktails within this publication, although for the home bar an extensive range of glassware is not always necessary. As an example, a wine glass could be used as a cocktail glass.

- ◆ **Cocktail**   90 ml (3 fl oz) – 140 ml (4⅔ fl oz)
- ◆ **Highball**   300 ml (10 fl oz)
- ◆ **Margarita**   260 ml (8⅔ fl oz)
- ◆ **Old-Fashioned**   180 ml (6 fl oz) – 290 ml (9⅔ fl oz)
- ◆ **Shot**   30 ml (1 fl oz) – 60 ml (2 fl oz)
- ◆ **Tall**   360 ml (12 fl oz)

MEASURES
1 dash   1 ml (⅟₃₀ fl oz)
1 teaspoon   5 ml (⅙ fl oz)
1 cup   250 ml (8⅓ fl oz)

COMMON INGREDIENTS FOR MARGARITA COCKTAILS

Spirits
Light Rum
Southern Comfort
Tequila
Vodka

Liqueurs
Amaretto / Curaçao
Apricot Brandy / Midori
Banana Liqueur
Strawberry Liqueur
Cointreau

COMMON MIXERS

- Apple Juice
- Lemon Juice
- Orange Juice
- Rose's Lime Juice Cordial
- Bitter-Lemon Soda
- Lime Juice

- Passionfruit Juice
- Sweet & Sour Mix
- Cranberry Juice
- Mineral Water
- Pineapple Juice
- Tomato Juice
- Eggs

GARNISHES AND ADDITIVES

- Apricots
- Kiwi Fruit
- Peaches
- Sugar
- Bananas

- Lemons
- Salt and Pepper
- Blackberries
- Limes
- Strawberries

◆ HOSTING A MARGARITA PARTY ◆

To be the host of a party can be stressful if you are not properly prepared. Here are some helpful hints to ensure that you and your guests enjoy the occasion.

It is advisable to pre-cut your fruit for garnishes and wrap them in plastic or place a clean damp linen cloth over them and refrigerate until required. Juices should be squeezed and/or removed from tin cans. Pour juices into resealable containers and refrigerate. Make up a bowl of sugar syrup as described under Useful Tips. This will save you from having to dissolve sugar when preparing large quantities of drinks.

Keep a glass of water on your bar for rinsing instruments such as spoons and stirrers. If your washing machine is in close proximity to your bar or kitchen, it can be used to fill with clean fresh ice.

If you find yourself hosting a large party, it is an idea to make yourself a checklist of what you require and what must be completed. Once your list is all checked off, you should then be able to sit down and relax before your home is invaded by guests. Then you can enjoy delectable Margarita cocktails with family and friends without the stress of hosting the occasion.

◆ CORDIALS AND LIQUEURS ◆

Cordials and liqueurs are essential ingredients in a vast variety of Margarita cocktails. They are alcohol-based with herbs, aromatic plants, essences, juices, beans, nuts, dairy products, sweeteners and colours which are infused in the spirit by the process of steeping and distillation.

Traditionally, cordials and liqueurs were created for medicinal purposes as a cure for all types of ills. Creating cordials and liqueurs hundreds of years ago meant that people would gather herbs, fruits and plants from their gardens, which they then added with sugar to liquors such as gin and brandy. Today cordials and liqueurs are produced by distilling companies worldwide. It would not be possible to list all cordials and liqueurs that are being produced or available. A list has been provided of the main ones that are required for Margarita recipes in the introduction of this book.

◆ TEQUILA ◆

Tequila is a Mexican spirit, although it is believed that the Aztecs drank pulque, an ancestor of tequila that's at least 2,000 years old.

Tequila is distilled from the blue Agave plant, which is also known as the Century plant. This plant resembles a large pineapple with spikes similar to the cactus plant, growing in abundance in the desert. When the plant reaches maturity (about ten years) the spikes are removed and the remainder of the plant is crushed to remove the sap (mescal). Sugar and yeast are then added to the mescal, which is then fermented for a few days and distilled twice in pot stills. Tequila is distilled in only two designated regions of Mexico, one being the surrounding area of Tequila and the other in the region of Tepatitlan.

There are two varieties of tequila; white or silver and gold. White tequila is aged for a very short period of time in wax-lined vats. Gold tequila is aged in whisky barrels for usually between two and four years until the spirit changes to a golden colour and is then ready to be bottled.

◆ MARGARITA ◆

The Margarita is a classic tequila-based cocktail and is certainly the most well known tequila cocktail worldwide.

It is uncertain who invented the Margarita cocktail and there are dozens of stories and theories behind origin of the Margarita. The most common belief is that this cocktail was invented in 1938 by Carlos Danny Herrera in his restaurant Rancho la Gloria situated between Tijuana and Rosarita, Mexico. It is believed that he created this cocktail for a guest Marjorie King who was allergic to most spirits but not allergic to tequila.

Another popular theory for the origin of the Margarita is that it was created by a socialite Margaret "Margarita" Sames in 1948 while holidaying in Acapulco.

The Margarita was first published in 1953 and appeared in an issue of *Esquire* magazine.

In 1977 Jimmy Buffet released the song "Margaritaville".

Today the Margarita has become a legendary tequila cocktail and there is an abundance of Margarita cocktail recipes available. The Margarita has come a long way since its original creation and now new versions of this drink are being created using a vast array of fresh fruits and juices.

The Margarita has become so popular worldwide that it has its own day – 22 February every year is National Margarita Day, which is an unofficial national holiday.

Margarita ——

COCKTAILS

CLASSIC MARGARITA

25.7% alc/vol

1.8 standard drinks

45 ml (1½ fl oz) gold tequila or white tequila
15 ml (½ fl oz) Cointreau
30 ml (1 fl oz) fresh lemon or lime juice
slice of fresh lemon

Prepare a margarita glass with a salt-frosted rim. Pour gold or white tequila as desired, Cointreau and lemon or lime juice as desired into a cocktail shaker over ice then shake well. Strain into prepared glass and garnish with a slice of lemon then serve.

BANANA MARGARITA

20.3% alc/vol
1.9 standard drinks

30 ml (1 fl oz) gold tequila
30 ml (1 fl oz) banana liqueur
15 ml (½ fl oz) Cointreau
30 ml (1 fl oz) fresh lemon juice
¼ fresh banana (diced)
slice of fresh banana

Prepare a margarita glass with a sugar-frosted rim moistened with lemon juice. Pour tequila, liqueur, Cointreau and juice into a blender over a large amount of crushed ice then add diced banana. Blend until slushy and pour into prepared glass. Garnish with a slice of banana and serve with a short straw.

APPLE MARGARITA

19.5% alc/vol
1.8 standard drinks

30 ml (1 fl oz) white tequila
30 ml (1 fl oz) Cointreau
60 ml (2 fl oz) apple juice

Pour ingredients into a cocktail shaker over ice and shake well.
Strain into a chilled margarita glass and serve.

BERRY MARGARITA

14.4% alc/vol
1.8 standard drinks

45 ml (1½ fl oz) white tequila
15 ml (½ fl oz) Cointreau
60 ml (2 fl oz) fresh lime juice
4 fresh strawberries (diced)
fresh strawberry

Prepare a margarita glass with a sugar-frosted rim. Pour tequila, Cointreau and juice into a blender over a large amount of crushed ice then add diced strawberries. Blend until slushy and pour into prepared glass. Garnish with a strawberry and serve.

CATALINA MARGARITA

13.5% alc/vol

2.4 standard drinks

45 ml (1½ fl oz) white tequila
30 ml (1 fl oz) Blue Curaçao
30 ml (1 fl oz) peach schnapps
120 ml (4 fl oz) sweet & sour mix

Pour ingredients into a cocktail shaker over ice and shake well. Strain into a chilled margarita glass and serve with a short straw.

MANDARIN MARGARITA

28.2% alc/vol

2.4 standard drinks

45ml (1½ fl oz) gold tequila
20ml (⅔ fl oz) Mandarine Napoleon
15ml (½ fl oz) Cointreau
30ml (1 fl oz) fresh lemon juice
slice of fresh orange

Prepare a margarita glass with a salt-frosted rim. Pour tequila, Mandarine Napoleon, Cointreau and juice into a blender over cracked ice then blend. Strain into prepared glass and garnish with a slice of orange then serve with a short straw.

SHARKARITA

25.4% alc/vol

1.9 standard drinks

45 ml (1½ fl oz) white tequila
15 ml (½ fl oz) Cointreau
5 ml (⅙ fl oz) raspberry liqueur
30 ml (1 fl oz) fresh lemon juice

Pour tequila, Cointreau and juice into a blender over a large amount of crushed ice then blend until slushy. Pour into a chilled margarita glass and gently add liqueur – do not stir, then serve.

TALL MARGARITA

11.4% alc/vol
1.8 standard drinks

45 ml (1½ fl oz) gold tequila
15 ml (½ fl oz) Cointreau
23 ml (¾ fl oz) fresh lemon juice
120 ml (4 fl oz) bitter-lemon soda
slice of fresh lemon

Pour tequila, Cointreau and juice into a cocktail shaker over ice then shake. Strain into a tall glass over ice and add bitter-lemon soda then stir gently. Add more ice to fill the glass and garnish with a slice of lemon then serve with a straw.

MANSION MARGARITA

26.9% alc/vol

2.6 standard drinks

38 ml (1¼ fl oz) gold tequila
23 ml (¾ fl oz) Cointreau
23 ml (¾ fl oz) Grand Marnier
38 ml (1¼ fl oz) sweet & sour mix

Pour ingredients into a cocktail shaker over ice and shake well. Strain into a margarita glass half-filled with cracked ice and add more cracked ice to fill the glass then serve with a short straw.

PINK MARGARITA

21.2% alc/vol

1.6 standard drinks

45 ml (1½ fl oz) white tequila
15 ml (½ fl oz) raspberry liqueur
5 ml (⅙ fl oz) grenadine
15 ml (½ fl oz) fresh lemon or lime juice
½ egg white

Prepare a margarita glass with a salt-frosted rim. Pour ingredients into a cocktail shaker over ice and shake well. Strain into prepared glass and serve.

GOLD MARGARITA

24% alc/vol
2.3 standard drinks

60 ml (2 fl oz) gold tequila
15 ml (½ fl oz) Cointreau
45 ml (1½ fl oz) fresh lime juice
wedge of fresh lime

Prepare a margarita glass with a salt-frosted rim. Pour tequila, Cointreau and juice into a cocktail shaker over ice then shake well. Strain into prepared glass and garnish with a wedge of lime then serve with a short straw.

MANGORITA

24% alc/vol
2.3 standard drinks

60 ml (2 fl oz) gold tequila
15 ml (½ fl oz) Cointreau
45 ml (1½ fl oz) mango nectar
wedge of fresh lime

Prepare a margarita glass with the rim moistened with lime juice and salt-frosted. Pour tequila, Cointreau and nectar into a blender over a large amount of crushed ice then blend until slushy. Pour into prepared glass and garnish with a wedge of lime then serve with a short straw.

WABORITA

26% alc/vol
3.7 standard drinks

60 ml (2 fl oz) gold tequila
60 ml (2 fl oz) Cointreau
60 ml (2 fl oz) fresh lime juice
slice of fresh lime

Prepare a margarita glass with a salt-frosted rim. Pour tequila, Cointreau and juice into a cocktail shaker over ice then shake well. Strain into prepared glass and garnish with a slice of lime then serve with a short straw.

BLACKBERRY MARGARITA

16.4% alc/vol

1.8 standard drinks

53 ml (1¾ fl oz) white tequila
15 ml (½ fl oz) blackberry schnapps
23 ml (¾ fl oz) fresh lime juice
10 fresh blackberries (diced)
2 fresh blackberries

Prepare a margarita glass with a sugar-frosted rim. Pour tequila, schnapps and juice into a blender over a large amount of crushed ice then add diced blackberries. Blend until slushy and pour into prepared glass. Garnish with blackberries and serve.

SOL-A-RITA

21.9% alc/vol

1.9 standard drinks

38 ml (1¼ fl oz) gold tequila
23 ml (¾ fl oz) Cointreau
2 dashes grenadine
45 ml (1½ fl oz) fresh orange juice

Pour ingredients into a cocktail shaker over ice and shake well. Strain into a margarita glass half-filled with cracked ice and add more cracked ice to fill the glass then serve with a short straw.

PINK CADILLAC MARGARITA

17.9% alc/vol
2.8 standard drinks

60 ml (2 fl oz) white tequila
30 ml (1 fl oz) Cointreau
60 ml (2 fl oz) fresh lime juice
30 ml (1 fl oz) cranberry juice
1 teaspoon sugar syrup

Pour ingredients into a cocktail shaker over small amount of cracked ice and shake well. Pour into a chilled margarita glass and serve with a short straw.

CADALAC MARGARITA

25.4% alc/vol

2.5 standard drinks

60 ml (2 fl oz) gold tequila
23 ml (¾ fl oz) Grand Marnier
38 ml (1¼ fl oz) sweet & sour mix
wedge of fresh lime

Prepare a margarita glass with a salt-frosted rim. Pour tequila, Grand Marnier and sweet & sour mix into a cocktail shaker over ice then shake well. Strain into prepared glass and garnish with a wedge of lime then serve.

COCO MARGARITA

12.5% alc/vol

1.4 standard drinks

38 ml (1¼ fl oz) white tequila
15 ml (½ fl oz) coconut liqueur
45 ml (1½ fl oz) pineapple juice
30 ml (1 fl oz) sweet & sour mix
15 ml (½ fl oz) fresh lime juice
slice of fresh pineapple

Prepare a margarita glass with a salt-frosted rim. Pour tequila, liqueur, juices and sweet & sour mix into a cocktail shaker over ice then shake well. Strain into prepared glass and garnish with a slice of pineapple then serve with a short straw.

BLUE MARGARITA

23.3% alc/vol

1.8 standard drinks

45 ml (1½ fl oz) white tequila
23 ml (¾ fl oz) blue curaçao
30 ml (1 fl oz) fresh lime juice

Prepare a margarita glass with a salt-frosted rim. Pour ingredients into a cocktail shaker over ice and shake well. Strain into prepared glass and serve with a short straw.

APRICOT MARGARITA

16.7% alc/vol
1.4 standard drinks

30 ml (1 fl oz) gold tequila
30 ml (1 fl oz) apricot brandy
45 ml (1½ fl oz) fresh lemon juice
1 teaspoon sugar syrup
slice of fresh apricot

Pour tequila, apricot brandy, juice and sugar into a cocktail shaker over ice then shake well. Strain into a chilled margarita glass and garnish with a slice of apricot then serve.

PEACH MARGARITA

13.5% alc/vol

1 standard drink

30 ml (1 fl oz) gold tequila
8 ml (¼ fl oz) peach liqueur
15 ml (½ fl oz) fresh lemon juice
½ fresh peach (diced)

Prepare a margarita glass with a sugar-frosted rim. Pour tequila, liqueur and juice into a blender over a large amount of crushed ice then add diced peach. Blend until slushy and pour into prepared glass then serve.

BLACKJACK MARGARITA

13.2% alc/vol
2 standard drinks

45 ml (1½ fl oz) white tequila
15 ml (½ fl oz) Chambord
15 ml (½ fl oz) Cointreau
120 ml (4 fl oz) fresh lime juice
wedge of fresh lime

Prepare a margarita glass with a salt-frosted rim. Pour tequila, Chambord, Cointreau and juice into a cocktail shaker over ice then shake well. Strain into prepared glass and garnish with a wedge of lime then serve with a short straw.

JIMPOP'S MARGARITA

28.4% alc/vol

2.5 standard drinks

60 ml (2 fl oz) gold tequila

23 ml (¾ fl oz) Grand Marnier

30 ml (1 fl oz) fresh lime juice

Prepare a margarita glass with a salt-frosted rim and half-fill the prepared glass with cracked ice. Pour ingredients into a mixing glass over ice and stir well. Strain into prepared glass and add more cracked ice to fill the glass then serve.

GOLDEN MARGARITA

27.7% alc/vol

2.3 standard drinks

45 ml (1½ fl oz) gold tequila
15 ml (½ fl oz) Cointreau
15 ml (½ fl oz) Grand Marnier
30 ml (1 fl oz) fresh lemon juice
Slice of fresh lemon

Prepare a margarita glass with a salt-frosted rim and half-fill the prepared glass with crushed ice. Pour tequila, Cointreau, Grand Marnier and juice into a cocktail shaker over ice then shake well. Strain into prepared glass and add more crushed ice to fill the glass. Garnish with a slice of lemon and serve.

GREEN IGUANA MARGARITA

13.9% alc/vol

1.2 standard drinks

30 ml (1 fl oz) white tequila
15 ml (½ fl oz) Midori
60 ml (2 fl oz) sweet & sour mix

Prepare a margarita glass with a salt-frosted rim. Pour ingredients into a blender over a large amount of cracked ice and blend. Pour into prepared glass and serve.

GRANRITA

25.7% alc/vol
1.8 standard drinks

45 ml (1½ fl oz) gold tequila
15 ml (½ fl oz) Grand Marnier
30 ml (1 fl oz) fresh lemon juice
slice of fresh lemon

Prepare a margarita glass with a salt-frosted rim and half-fill the prepared glass with crushed ice. Pour tequila, Grand Marnier and juice into a cocktail shaker over ice then shake well. Strain into prepared glass and add more crushed ice to fill the glass then stir. Garnish with a slice of lemon and serve with a short straw.

MARGARITA SHOOTER

26% alc/vol

0.9 standard drinks

15 ml (½ fl oz) Cointreau

15 ml (½ fl oz) gold tequila

10 ml (⅓ fl oz) fresh lemon juice

5 ml (⅙ fl oz) fresh lime juice

Layer ingredients in order given into a shot glass and serve as a shooter.

FUZZY RITA

21.8% alc/vol

2.1 standard drinks

45 ml (1½ fl oz) gold tequila
15 ml (½ fl oz) Cointreau
15 ml (½ fl oz) peach schnapps
45 ml (1½ fl oz) fresh lime juice

Pour ingredients into a mixing glass over ice and stir well. Strain into an old-fashioned glass over ice and add more ice to fill the glass then serve with a short straw.

LA JOLLARITA

34.1% alc/vol

2 standard drinks

45 ml (1½ fl oz) white tequila
15 ml (½ fl oz) Chambord
15 ml (½ fl oz) Cointreau

Pour ingredients into a cocktail shaker over ice and shake.
Strain into a chilled margarita glass and serve.

CHINA DYNASTY MARGARITA

21.3% alc/vol
1.8 standard drinks

30 ml (1 fl oz) gold tequila
30 ml (1 fl oz) Cointreau
30 ml (1 fl oz) fresh lime juice
15 ml (½ fl oz) fresh lemon juice
1 teaspoon sugar syrup
wedge of fresh lime

Prepare a margarita glass with a salt-frosted rim. Pour tequila, Cointreau, juices and sugar into a blender over a large amount of crushed ice then blend until slushy. Pour into prepared glass and garnish with a wedge of lime then serve with a short straw.

STRAWBERRY MARGARITA

20.3% alc/vol

2 standard drinks

45 ml (1½ fl oz) white tequila
15 ml (½ fl oz) Cointreau
8 ml (¼ fl oz) strawberry liqueur
15 ml (½ fl oz) fresh lemon juice
4 fresh strawberries (diced)
fresh strawberry

Prepare a margarita glass with a sugar-frosted rim. Pour tequila, Cointreau, liqueur and juice into a blender over a large amount of crushed ice then add diced strawberries. Blend until slushy and pour into prepared glass. Garnish with a strawberry and serve with a short straw.

JAGERITA

24.4% alc/vol

0.6 standard drinks

10 ml (⅓ fl oz) Jägermeister
10 ml (⅓ fl oz) gold tequila
10 ml (⅓ fl oz) fresh lime juice

Pour ingredients in order given gently into a shot glass – do not stir, then serve as a shooter.

BANANA MARGARITA NO.2

17.2% alc/vol

1.6 standard drinks

45 ml (1½ fl oz) white tequila

15 ml (½ fl oz) banana liqueur

30 ml (1 fl oz) fresh lime juice

½ fresh banana (diced)

slice of fresh banana

Prepare a margarita glass with a sugar-frosted rim – moistened with lime juice. Pour tequila, liqueur and juice into a blender over a large amount of crushed ice then add diced banana. Blend until slushy and pour into prepared glass. Garnish with a slice of banana and serve with a short straw.

SOUTHERN TRADITION MARGARITA

11% alc/vol

2 standard drinks

45 ml (1½ fl oz) gold tequila
23 ml (¾ fl oz) Southern Comfort
15 ml (½ fl oz) fresh lime juice
150 ml (5 fl oz) sweet & sour mix
wedge of fresh lime

Pour tequila, Southern Comfort, juice and sweet & sour mix into a cocktail shaker over ice then shake well. Strain into a tall glass over ice and more ice to fill the glass. Add a wedge of lime and serve with a straw.

PASSIONATE RITA

25.7% alc/vol
1.8 standard drinks

45 ml (1½ fl oz) gold tequila
30 ml (1 fl oz) passionfruit liqueur
15 ml (½ fl oz) fresh lime juice

Pour ingredients into a cocktail shaker over ice and shake well.
Strain into a chilled cocktail glass and serve with a short straw.

CHAMORITA

4.5% alc/vol

1 standard drink

20 ml (⅔ fl oz) vodka
10 ml (⅓ fl oz) apricot brandy
10 ml (⅓ fl oz) orange curaçao
10 ml (⅓ fl oz) fresh orange Juice
10 ml (⅓ fl oz) passionfruit juice
210 ml (7 fl oz) mineral water
slice of fresh orange

Pour vodka, apricot brandy, curaçao and juices into a cocktail shaker over ice then shake well. Strain into a chilled highball glass and add mineral water then stir gently. Garnish with a slice of orange and serve with a straw.

SANGRITA NO.2

30 ml (1 fl oz) tomato juice (chilled)
dash fresh lemon juice
pinch of black pepper (ground)

Pour juices into a mixing glass over ice and add black pepper to the mixing glass then stir well. Strain into a chilled shot glass and serve; to be slowly sipped.

FROZEN STRAWBERRY MARGARITA

21.9% alc/vol
1.8 standard drinks

35 ml (1⅙ fl oz) white tequila
20 ml (⅔ fl oz) strawberry liqueur
20 ml (⅔ fl oz) triple sec
20 ml (⅔ fl oz) Rose's Lime Juice cordial
10 ml (⅓ fl oz) fresh lemon juice

Pour ingredients into a mixing glass without ice and stir well. Pour into a margarita glass half-filled with crushed and shaved ice. Add more crushed and shaved ice to fill the glass then serve with 2 short straws.

This drink is also known as a Peckerhead.

BAJA MARGARITA

17.7% alc/vol

2.5 standard drinks

60 ml (2 fl oz) gold tequila

30 ml (1 fl oz) Damiana liqueur

90 ml (3 fl oz) fresh lime juice

Prepare a margarita glass with a salt-frosted rim. Pour ingredients into a cocktail shaker over small amount of cracked ice and shake well. Pour into prepared glass and serve with a short straw.

MARGATINI

34.2% alc/vol
1.6 standard drinks

45 ml (1½ fl oz) white tequila
15 ml (½ fl oz) orange curaçao
dash fresh lime juice

Pour ingredients into a cocktail shaker over ice and shake.
Strain into a chilled margarita glass and serve.

SANGRITA

18.7% alc/vol

0.9 standard drinks

30 ml (1 fl oz) gold tequila or white tequila
30 ml (1 fl oz) tomato juice (chilled)
dash fresh lemon juice
pinch of black pepper (ground)

This drink is served with the tequila in its own shot glass and the other ingredients are mixed together and served in a separate chilled shot glass. The drinker takes a sip of the tequila and then a sip from the other shot glass until all is consumed. First pour gold or white tequila into a shot glass. Then pour juices into a mixing glass over ice followed by black pepper. Stir well and strain into a chilled shot glass then serve together with the tequila in the (unchilled) shot glass.

TINA RITA

32% alc/vol
1.6 standard drinks

38 ml (1¼ fl oz) vodka
8 ml (¼ fl oz) Cointreau
8 ml (¼ fl oz) Grand Marnier
5 ml (⅙ fl oz) fresh lime juice
5 ml (⅙ fl oz) sweet & sour mix
wedge of fresh lime

Prepare a margarita glass with a salt and sugar-frosted rim
– moistened with sweet & sour mix. Pour vodka, Cointreau,
Grand Marnier, juice and sweet & sour mix into a cocktail
shaker over ice then shake well. Strain into prepared glass and
garnish with a wedge of lime then serve with a short straw.

ITALIAN MARGARITA

14.9% alc/vol
1.4 standard drinks

30 ml (1 fl oz) amaretto
15 ml (½ fl oz) gold tequila
15 ml (½ fl oz) triple sec
60 ml (2 fl oz) sweet & sour mix

Pour ingredients into a chilled margarita glass and stir well. Add ice to fill the glass and stir gently then serve with a short straw.

MIDORI MARGARITA

16.1% alc/vol
1.4 standard drinks

30 ml (1fl oz) white tequila
30 ml (1fl oz) Midori
45 ml (1½ fl oz) fresh lemon juice
1 teaspoon sugar syrup
slice of fresh lime

Pour tequila, Midori, juice and sugar into a cocktail shaker over ice then shake well. Strain into a chilled margarita glass and garnish with a slice of lime then serve.

RED RITA

16.7% alc/vol
1.5 standard drinks

30 ml (1 fl oz) white tequila
30 ml (1 fl oz) white curaçao
45 ml (1½ fl oz) cranberry juice
8 ml (¼ fl oz) fresh lime juice

Pour ingredients into a cocktail shaker over ice and shake well.
Strain into a chilled old-fashioned glass and serve.

ELECTRIC MARGARITA

27.8% alc/vol

1.6 standard drinks

45 ml (1½ fl oz) white tequila
15 ml (½ fl oz) blue curaçao
15 ml (½ fl oz) Rose's Lime Juice cordial
wedge of fresh lime

Prepare a margarita glass with a salt-frosted rim. Pour tequila, curaçao and juice into a cocktail shaker over ice then shake. Strain into prepared glass and garnish with a wedge of lime then serve with a short straw.

RUMARITA

30.8% alc/vol
1.8 standard drinks

45 ml (1½ fl oz) light rum
15 ml (½ fl oz) Cointreau
15 ml (½ fl oz) fresh lime juice

Prepare a margarita glass with a course salt-frosted rim and half-fill the prepared glass with crushed ice. Pour ingredients into a cocktail shaker over ice and shake. Strain into prepared glass and serve with a short straw.

KIWI MARGARITA

17.5% alc/vol

2.1 standard drinks

45 ml (1½ fl oz) white tequila
15 ml (½ fl oz) Cointreau
15 ml (½ fl oz) Midori
15 ml (½ fl oz) fresh lemon juice
1 fresh kiwi fruit (diced)
slice of fresh kiwi fruit
slice of fresh orange

Prepare a margarita glass with a sugar-frosted rim. Pour tequila, Cointreau, Midori and juice into a blender over a large amount of crushed ice then add diced kiwi fruit. Blend until slushy and pour into prepared glass. Garnish with a slice of kiwi fruit and orange then serve.

PECKERHEAD

21.9% alc/vol
1.8 standard drinks

This drink is also known as Frozen Strawberry Margarita (pg 110).

FROZEN MARGARITA

13% alc/vol
1.8 standard drinks

This drink is a Margarita that is blended with a large amount of crushed ice until slushy. Please see Classic Margarita (pg 25).

Frozen Margarita

Glossary

Amaretto Almond-flavoured liqueur that originated from Italy in 1525................................. `28`

Apricot Brandy Apricot-flavoured brandy.. `23`

Banana Liqueur Banana-flavoured liqueur.. `23`

Chambord Black raspberry-flavoured liqueur produced in the Burgundy region of France.........
.... `16.5`

Coconut Liqueur Coconut-flavoured liqueur with a light rum-base....................................... `23`

Cointreau Sweet orange-flavoured liqueur that is colourless and arguably the world's
finest Triple Sec. It has been produced by the Cointreau family in France since 1849...... `40`

Curaçao Sweet orange-flavoured liqueur produced from curaçao orange peel.It is available
in six varieties: blue, green, orange, red, white (clear) and yellow.................................... `25`

Damiana Liqueur Light herbal-based liqueur produced in Mexico and created from the
damiana herb... `30`

Grand Marnier Orange-flavoured Cognac-based liqueur produced in France and created
in 1880. It is available in two varieties: red ribbon and yellow ribbon – red ribbon has a
higher % alc/vol at 40% alc/vol.. `40`

Grenadine Sweet red syrup, flavoured with pomegranate juice... `Nil`

Jägermeister Herb liqueur produced in Germany from 56 herbs, fruits and roots.
Originally created in 1934 by Curt Mast and the recipe still remains a secret.................... `35`

Mandarine Napoleon Mandarin-flavoured Belgian liqueur with a Cognac-base and is
produced from mandarin (tangerine) peels.. `40`

Midori Brand name of a honeydew melon-flavoured liqueur that is green in colour and produced by the Suntory Distilling Company in Japan. **21**

Passionfruit Liqueur Passionfruit-flavoured liqueur produced from Passionfruit. **20**

Peach Liqueur Peach-flavoured liqueur. **23**

Raspberry Liqueur Raspberry-flavoured liqueur. **20**

Rum (Light) Spirit aged for approximately six to twelve months in oak casks after being distilled in a column-still, which produces clear spirit. Originally produced in the southern Caribbean Islands. **38**

Schnapps Generic name for flavoured alcohol that is produced from grain or potato mash. Schnapps can be very sweet through to dry with many varieties available. % alc/vol content varies between the varieties. 20% alc/vol is average for commercial Schnapps. **20**

Southern Comfort Peach-flavoured liqueur that is brandy and bourbon-based. Created by M.W. Heron in New Orleans over one hundred years ago. **37**

Strawberry Liqueur Strawberry-flavoured liqueur. **23**

Tequila Spirit distilled from the sap of the dessert dwelling agave plant in Mexico. **38**

Triple Sec Orange-flavoured liqueur produced from orange peel – also referred to as curaçao. **25**

Vodka Clear, odourless and tasteless spirit distilled from fermented grain mash and filtered through charcoal. Traditional Russian and Polish vodkas have subtle aromas and flavours. **37**

Index

A

Apple Margarita 29
Apricot Margarita 67

B

Baja Margarita 111
Banana Margarita 27
Banana Margarita No.2 98
Berry Margarita 31
Blackberry Margarita 53
Blackjack Margarita 73
Blue Margarita 65

C

Cadalac Margarita 61
Catalina Margarita 33
Chamorita 105
China Dynasty Margarita 93
Classic Margarita 25
Coco Margarita 63

E

Electric Margarita 125

F

Frozen Margarita 133
Frozen Strawberry Margarita 110
Fuzzy Rita 89

G

Golden Margarita 79
Gold Margarita 49
Granrita 83
Green Iguana Margarita 81

I

Italian Margarita 117

J

Jagerita 97
Jimpop's Margarita 75

K

Kiwi Margarita 131

L

La Jollarita 92

M

Mandarin Margarita 37
Mangorita 50
Mansion Margarita 43
Margarita Shooter 85
Margatini 113
Midori Margarita 121

P

Passionate Rita 103
Peach Margarita 71
Peckerhead 133
Pink Cadillac Margarita 59
Pink Margarita 47

R

Red Rita 123
Rumarita 129

S

Sangrita 115
Sangrita No.2 107
Sharkarita 39
Sol-a-Rita 55
Southern Tradition Margarita 99
Strawberry Margarita 95

T

Tall Margarita 41
Tina Rita 116

W

Waborita 51

First published in 2017 by New Holland Publishers
London • Sydney • Auckland

The Chandlery 50 Westminster Bridge Road London SE1 7QY United Kingdom
1/66 Gibbes Street Chatswood NSW 2067 Australia
5/39 Woodside Ave Northcote, Auckland 0627 New Zealand

www.newhollandpublishers.com

A record of this book is held at the British Library and the National Library of Australia.

ISBN 9781742579412

Group Managing Director: Fiona Schultz
Publisher: Alan Whiticker
Project Editor: Sarah Menary
Designer: Lorena Susak
Proof Reader: Kaitlyn Smith
Production Director: James Mills-Hicks
Special thanks to Chris Howley for making the cocktails
Printer: Hang Tai Printing Company Limited

10 9 8 7 6 5 4 3 2 1

Keep up with New Holland Publishers on Facebook
www.facebook.com/NewHollandPublishers